TV TODAY

by Grace

SCHOLASTIC BOOK SERVICES
New York Toronto London Auckland Sydney Tokyo

Acknowledgments

I would like to thank Eve Ronan for her contributions to the Tom Selleck chapter and Sonia Black for hers to the chapter on Lisa Whelchel.

Photo Credits: Paramount Television: Cover, pp. 4-5, 7, 11, 13, 15, 17, 19, 23, 24-25, 27, 77, 81, 100; RCA: p. 30; Embassy Television: pp. 33, 37; Atari: p. 42; T.A.T. Communications: Cover, pp. 51, 53, 55; Kramer & Reiss Public Relations: p. 63; Universal Television: Cover, pp. 66, 71, 83, 85; Warner Bros. Television: p. 91; Columbia Pictures Television: pp. 93, 95; Tandem Productions, Inc.: p. 103.

Pac-Man is a trademark of Midway Manufacturing Company.

ISBN 0-590-32815-8

12 11 10 9 8 7 6 5 4 3 2 1   1   3 4 5 6/8

To Mom, Dad, Michelle, and Steve.

TABLE OF

CONTENTS

TV Today Is Hollywood! It's series, soap operas, sports, variety shows, and movies. It's *Magnum, P.I.*, *The Dukes of Hazzard, Hill Street Blues*, and *Happy Days*. It's Scott Baio, Lisa Whelchel, Gary Coleman, and Lee Majors.

BUT THAT'S NOT ALL! TV TODAY IS MUCH MORE!

TV Today Is Cable! It's sports channels, music channels, culture channels, weather channels. It's recently released movies without commercials. It's two-way TV you can talk back to!

TV Today Is Video Games! It's a baseball park, a football stadium, and an intergalactic battleground. It's Atari, Intellivision, PlayCable, and ColecoVision! It's Donkey Kong, Defender, Asteroids, Pac-Man, and Missile Command!

TURN THE PAGE AND TUNE IN TO THE NEW TV TODAY!

HOW SCOTT BAIO MANAGES

If you're the kind of *Happy Days* fan who has never missed a single episode, Chachi Arcola is as familiar to you as the boy next door. And if you're that same die-hard *Happy Days* fan and now a *Joanie Loves Chachi* fan, too, you'll know that the actor who plays Chachi is Scott Baio.

Will the real Scott Baio please stand up?

Scott Baio and Chachi Arcola have the same face and they have the same voice, but how else are they alike? And how are they different? Since Chachi doesn't like to give interviews, I went to Scott to find the answers.

"It's easier if the character you're playing has some of you in it," Scott told me, "so I just put a little bit of me in him, little reactions here and there. But most of the time, he's just a character. He's not that close to me.

"Chachi is on his own. Because he's had no father, he's smarter and more streetwise than I am," Scott explained. "I think that's the difference . . . And he's in love and I'm not!"

Does Scott ever wish he were more like Chachi?

"No," Scott answered. "I'm happy being me, and I think he's all right being him."

Scott may feel he doesn't have much more in common with Chachi than a few reactions here and there and an uncanny physical resemblance, but Scott feels that Chachi is basically an okay guy.

"He's very direct," Scott explained. "He doesn't beat around the bush. He tells you, 'I like this,' or 'I don't like this.' He tells you what he's thinking and he tells you how he feels, and I think that's good!"

Chachi is only one of many characters that Scott has played. It all started when Scott told his mother he wanted to be on TV.

"She took me to a couple of people in the city [New York], and they started sending me on interviews and that was it! I got lucky!"

Scott's luck led him to modeling jobs and commercials and then his first big role as the lead in an all-kid cast of the movie *Bugsy Malone*. That was followed by roles in four TV series (*Blansky's Beauties*, *Who's Watching the Kids?*, *Happy Days*, and *Joanie Loves Chachi*), three movies (*Foxes*, *Skatetown U.S.A.*, and *The Whiz Kid*), five TV movie specials, and a play for cable TV. And if that weren't enough, Scott has also cut a solo record album!

Whew! Does that sound impressive? It sure is! But there's one person who isn't impressed. That person is Scott himself. As strange as it may seem to his fans, Scott is his own worst critic.

"I very rarely like anything I do," he said. "The only two things I like are a TV movie I did about two years ago called *The Boy Who Drank Too Much* and a play I did for cable TV called *Gemini*."

3

Life with Father

What do Scott Baio and the Baltimore Orioles have in common? They both have great managers! Scott's manager is most special of all. That's because Scott's manager is his dad. How does that work out?

"It's really good because he looks out for me," Scott said. "When I get a script, we talk about it and think it out. He doesn't care about the money. He cares about what's good for me. That's all that counts.

"The agent gets you the job," Scott explained. "Then the manager sets up everything else. He handles all the details and takes care of the little things that will make you comfortable when you're working.

"Sometimes you work fifteen or sixteen hours a day on a movie, and at that point, you don't even realize that you're tired. You sort of go into a different state of mind. It's sort of like *The Twilight Zone*. Then your manager says, 'Okay, you should cool it now.'"

How does Scott unwind after a hard day's night?

"I play guitar. I watch a lot of TV. I watch reruns of *Kojak* every day, twice a day! It's my favorite show! On Saturdays and Sundays, I love to watch all the boxing matches and all of the other sporting events.

"I go to arcades once in a great while. I was *really* into that for a while. I used to drop quarters left and right and then I stopped."

What's up next, Scott?

Scott couldn't say too much about his future plans because he was in the middle of making some deals. But he did tell us about two of his personal goals. One of his dreams is to direct a film.

"When you're an actor, the only thing you're concerned with is yourself and the other people in the scene with you. But there are a million things that go on behind a camera, and it's so fascinating! When you're behind the camera you concern yourself with the actors, the lighting, everything! Is there a light glaring off the glass? Is his hair in his eyes? Is he on his mark?

"During the last film I did, when I wasn't on camera, I was behind the camera. I even operated a few shots!"

Scott's other dream is to play Billy the Kid.

"I'd like to be a cowboy," he said. "It's a big fantasy of mine to do a Western with the guns and the hats and the spurs. Riding into town and having a shoot-out — that's what I want to do!"

And with those last words, Scott rode off into the sunset. Happy days . . . er . . . trails, pardner!

ERIN MORAN TALKS ABOUT GROWING UP ON TV

Erin Moran has spent almost half her life as Joanie Cunningham. When *Happy Days* premiered in 1974, Erin was twelve years old. She was the only kid among a cast of adults. Erin isn't a kid anymore. She has grown up—and into her own TV show, *Joanie Loves Chachi*. In this conversation, Erin told me what growing up on TV has been like for her.

"People always come up to me and say, 'You know, I grew up with you,' and they love it. I can see it in their faces. I'm like part of their families. It's neat! It's a really nice thing to go through!"

Erin began acting in commercials at age five. Her first television role was in a pilot called *Stanley vs. the System*, and her first movie role was in *How Sweet It Is* with Debbie Reynolds. From 1968 to 1969, Erin was in *Daktari*, a popular TV series about an American family studying animals in Africa.

Anson Williams, Erin's costar in a Hallmark Hall of Fame production called *Lisa Bright and Dark*, encouraged her to try out for *Happy Days*. That was the beginning of a nine-year job!

Erin had a tutor while she worked. When she wasn't working, Erin attended Walter Reed Junior High School and then North Hollywood High School.

Six-year-old Erin in *Daktari*

"I didn't really enjoy school, because I wasn't in it much. I was in and out so much that I couldn't get into sports and cheerleading and all that."

It was difficult to make friends, and Erin missed having kids her own age to talk to.

The only kid on the block

"I was the only child for the first two or three years of the show," Erin said. "Until Scott came along, I had no one my age who knew what I was going through. It was hard growing up. The rest of the cast was so much older than me.

"I had so many people watching out for me, which is fabulous, but it got a little hard." Erin explained, "Not only did I have my parents guiding me, but I had parents at the studio guiding me. I never got away from it.

"I always wanted to be an adult. At fifteen, I was already eighteen in my mind. I wanted to be on my own."

In addition to being the youngest member of the *Happy Days* cast, Erin is the youngest member of her real family, where there are six kids. Erin's family life, however, was very different from Joanie's.

"The Cunninghams are very understanding. There were arguments, but they realized what Joanie was going through," Erin explained. "There was always a happy ending.

"I was raised very strict. I could never get away with what Joanie got away with on the show. Forget

about it! When I was younger, I would never get out of line and tell my parents how I felt.

"My parents would always say, 'No,' and I would say, 'Why?' But they would never give me a reason. My parents were set in their ways.

"Because I was in show business, they were afraid something bad would happen to me. Now I know the ins and outs of the business. I know how far I can go and how far I can't go. I'm careful. All in all, they did a great job."

Joanie meets Chachi

When Scott Baio joined the *Happy Days* cast in 1977, it meant a big change for Erin. Scott had a big effect on both her personal life and her professional life.

"He's my best friend," Erin said. "He knows me better than anybody. He's been there when I've needed him, and I've been there when he's needed me. That's what a best friend is all about!

"If Scott had left *Happy Days*, it would have been a tragedy for me. It would have been really hard, because he's my partner. I play off him, and he plays off me."

Their partnership came off so well on *Happy Days* that the producers decided to give Erin and Scott their own show, *Joanie Loves Chachi.*

"The idea came up two years ago when Scott and I sang our first song on *Happy Days*," Erin said. "They saw that it clicked, and they went on from there. We tried four shows—and now we're a hit!"

CATHY SILVERS— A SECOND-GENERATION STAR!

Happy Days fans heard about her for years—but they never saw her. Her name is Jenny Piccalo, and she's Joanie Cunningham's best friend. From Joanie's description, you'd know that Jenny was supposed to be an outgoing, boy-crazy blonde bombshell. In 1980 Jenny was actually written into the show. The search was on to find someone who would fit Jenny's well-known description. Everyone knew exactly what they were looking for. Then Cathy Silvers showed up and changed everyone's mind.

"I hate to say it, but I didn't watch Happy Days," Cathy said. "I didn't know who Jenny Piccalo was, and I didn't know what she was all about. Maybe that was fortunate. If I had known she was supposed to be some great thing, I would have gone in with a negative attitude. But I didn't. I went in thinking that possibly I could be like this girl."

As Cathy returned for auditions, she noticed that everyone in the waiting room looked the same . . . except for her.

"It was weird," Cathy explained. "I would go in and see all these blonde bombshells. I asked my agent, 'What am I doing there? Come on. Send me on something else. I don't belong there.' I felt so inferior.

"I started getting the feeling after a while that they were using me as a last resort. If they couldn't find what they were looking for, then they were going to go with me.

"I'd go in there, and they'd laugh, and I'd do the same part, the same script, every day over and over for I don't know how long! I don't know how many times I went back. I kept getting skinnier and skinnier and more and more nervous. I thought, 'This is ridiculous,' and then one day I got it!"

When Cathy first got the part, she and her character seemed very similar. "I'm not quiet and I'm not shy, and neither is Jenny," Cathy said. "I'm not outspoken, but I speak my mind, and so does Jenny."

As time went on and the writers developed the character more, Cathy saw many differences between herself and Jenny.

"Jenny is erratic, boy-crazy, a troublemaker, the loud one in the bunch," Cathy said. "She's a schemer, probably not too secure, probably not sure about what's right and what's wrong. She tries to do good, but it never seems to work out that way.

"The longer they wrote Jenny, the more the separation began, and the older I get, the less I am like Jenny," Cathy added. "I don't think there are too many similarities between us. I'm not wild. I'm not crazy. I'm not boy-crazy. I don't speak out when I'm not supposed to."

Following in Dad's footsteps

One of the funniest characters on TV during the late fifties was Master Sergeant Ernie Bilko. Bilko could outtalk, outmanuever, and outscheme anyone who was lucky enough to be stationed at Fort Baxter. Bilko was played by Cathy's dad, Phil Silvers.

"People say, 'Did you study Bilko? Did you watch it? What did it do for your acting career?' And really, it didn't have an effect. I was too young," Cathy explained.

"My parents didn't make it a big deal. Mom didn't say, 'Okay, everybody in front of the TV. Dad's on!' We'd never watch him for that long. It became boring. We'd watch him for a while, and then if something else took our attention away, it was no big deal because he was on every week.

"It would be like any other kid watching Daddy at work. A father could be the President of the United States, and to a kid, it's just Daddy. That's how it was for us."

During one episode of *Happy Days*, Jenny Piccalo's father made an appearance. Guess who played the part! Phil Silvers!

"That was scary," Cathy said. "I was really nervous. I thought he was going to do something wrong or say something he shouldn't. I thought it wouldn't work. I just thought of all the things that could happen. I was so nervous, but it worked. It all came together in the end."

What made the show especially fun was that there was a lot of Bilko in Mr. Piccalo. A fast-talker who was full of flattering words, Jenny's dad brought back memories of those happy days when *The Phil Silvers Show* was on TV.

Secret of success

How did Cathy prepare for her career? By studying speech in high school.

"I think that's what gave me my basic training," Cathy said. "Not too many kids are involved in the public speaking and forensics teams and tournaments that go on in high school. It's really un-

fortunate. But that's not really the kids' fault, because not too many high schools have it.

"A lot of times when I say forensics, people think I'm talking about dead bodies. They have no idea what I'm talking about. In the meantime, I got the greatest training I ever could have asked for as far as learning how to memorize lines, competing, traveling, and exploring my talents.

"By the time I went to audition for *Happy Days*, I'd stood up in front of more people than I could ever remember. I'd taken a script and read it in front of an audience. I learned how to touch emotions and make the joke and hit feelings in comedy and in drama. When I walked in and had to do that for *Happy Days*, I just put myself in the same situation—and it paid off!"

Back to school

Cathy has only one regret. "I want to go back to school," she said. "Surprise, surprise! I was very anti-college before. I didn't want to go. I wanted to work."

What made her want to go back?

"Lack of education," she answered. "Seeing all my friends getting smarter. I lose out on their conversations. They're so much ahead of me, and that's bad. It makes me feel dumb and uneducated. I'm becoming aware of how important college is. Before, I didn't think it was a big deal. Now I want to go. I want to hit the books!"

HENRY WINKLER GETS HIS MESSAGE ACROSS

When *Happy Days* began in 1974, the Fonz was just a minor character who received fifth billing. Henry Winkler turned the Fonz into the most popular character on *Happy Days* and the hippest hero in the world! In this interesting question-and-answer session I had with him, he explained how he did it!

What makes the Fonz so cool?

What I think makes the Fonz so cool is that he respects himself. He can care for other people around him. He can care about how other people feel. It's not just a way of acting. It's a way of being.

Do his motorcycle and his leather jacket make the Fonz cool?

No, that's just his life-style.

Did you yourself ever dress like that?

No. I went to a private school when I went to high school. I wore a jacket and tie to school every day.

What do you like best about the Fonz?

Well, I like the way the Fonz stands up on his own two feet. I like that the Fonz never uses violence. I like the way the Fonz is so loyal to his friends.

Do you know anyone like the Fonz?

No.

Are you anything like the Fonz?

No . . . except we're both cute.

If you aren't anything like the Fonz and you don't know anyone like the Fonz, how have you managed to make the Fonz so real and so special?

Well, it came from my imagination. It came from who I would like this guy to be. From the beginning, I worked on the details. I'd go home and do homework. I'd study the script and figure out what I could do to make the Fonz original.

So you used what you learned at acting school?

Every moment of training that I had is included in the Fonz. Every moment of the nine years that I went to drama school is in the Fonz.

Did you always want to be an actor?

Since I was seven years old.

What made you decide you wanted to be an actor?
That I can't tell you. I don't know. If people were born to do things, then I was born to do this.

What did you do when you decided to be an actor?
I knew that there were lots of actors around, and that education was most important. I went to

school, and then I went to college, and then I went to graduate school. I studied liberal arts along with drama. I knew that if I didn't make a living as an actor, I'd have my education to fall back on. Anyway, it's important for an actor to know a lot of things.

Do you have anything to do with writing the scripts for Happy Days?

Yes, I have a lot to do with it. Monday mornings, we read the script around the table. The actors and the directors and the producers get together, and we all say what we feel about that week's story.

Have you ever said, "This isn't good. I don't like it at all"?

Many, many, many, many times. Nobody knows the character like the actor who plays him.

Have you ever come up with any ideas for Happy Days *stories?*

There was one where Richie was in a car accident and almost died. I went to visit him in the hospital, and that was the first time anyone ever saw the Fonz cry. That was my idea. I wanted to show that you could cry and still be cool. If we weren't sup-

posed to cry, we wouldn't have tear ducts. Also, I was the chairman of the Epilepsy Foundation for some time, so I suggested a story where we showed that people with epilepsy can get along very well in the world.

So you can use your role as the Fonz to say things you want to say to people?

Yeah, without a doubt! There was a time when I said to Richie that it was cool to have a library card. Registration for library cards went up five hundred percent all over the country!

The Fonz has gone through a lot of changes over the years. In the beginning of the show, he was a high school dropout who worked as a garage mechanic. Now he has earned his diploma, and he teaches high school shop. How do you feel about the changes the Fonz has gone through over the years?

Well, I like the changes. They keep the character interesting, so I don't get bored.

How did you feel when Ron Howard and Scott Baio left the show?

Well, Ronnie had to leave because he had to meet his destiny. Scott was ready to go off on his own. He goes to class; he studies mime. He trained himself. He established himself as a good actor.

Do you still keep in touch with them?

Oh, yes. Scottie and I are still good friends. As a matter of fact, Ronnie Howard directed me in a film.

If you could create any movie role for yourself, what would that be?

I'd like to act with E.T. *E.T.* is one of the greatest movies ever made. I wept throughout that film. I love E.T.

Do you plan to do any new movies soon?

Not at the moment. I'm getting ready to do the tenth year of *Happy Days*.

Are you excited about that?

Sure!

What will happen to the Fonz this year?

I think this year he's going to have a girl friend who plays the flute. She has a child from a previous marriage.

Will the Fonz get married?

I don't know. But if the Fonz ever got married, he'd marry an English professor, because I think opposites attract. That would be really interesting!

If the Fonz and Henry Winkler met, what would the Fonz think of Henry Winkler?

Oh, I think he would want to take me out to dinner!

Did you ever expect it to last this long?

Never! Never!

Do you read your fan mail?

I read a lot of it. Other people help me read it, or I wouldn't be able to do the show! And everyone who writes gets a picture.

TV YESTERDAY

Tune In To 1946!

Here's what you would have seen if you had turned on your TV set any evening in 1946!

	DUMONT	NBC
Sunday		
8:00	Movie	Face to Face
8:15		Geographically Speaking
8:30		Television Screen Magazine
Monday		
7:45		Newsreel
8:00		Voice of Firestone Televues
9:00		Gillette Cavalcade of Sports
Tuesday		
8:00	Play the Game	
9:00	Serving Through Science	
Wednesday		
9:00	Faraway Hill	

DUMONT   NBC

Thursday

7:45		Newsreel
8:00		Hour Glass
9:00	Cash and Carry	

Friday

8:15		You Are an Artist
8:30		I Love to Eat
8:45		Voice of Firestone
		Televues
9:30		Gillette Cavalcade of
		Sports

MEET SQUARE PEG AMY LINKER

Lauren Hutchinson of CBS-TV's *Square Pegs* is never at a loss for words. Neither is Amy Linker, the actress who plays Lauren. See if you agree as you read the fast-paced question-and-answer session I had with her.

Congratulations! Square Pegs is a wonderful show!
Thanks! I think so, too!

How would you describe Lauren in a few words?
She's very romantic. She's very bright and intelligent. She has a lot of energy. She's very into boys.

What are her weaknesses?
Her weakness for food, her impatience. She's very aggressive, very assertive. She tries to make herself look good with crazy hairstyles that she thinks are really in, but the socialites think she's really tacky.

Lauren wears braces, but you're not wearing braces.

Actually, I always wanted to. All my friends were getting braces, and I thought it made them special, so I wanted them, too. I wanted to be like my friends.

How would you describe yourself in a few words?

I'd say I'm a lot like Lauren. I'm aggressive, except I don't show it as much as Lauren does. I like school. I like acting a lot. I love boys. I'm dying for a boyfriend — just like Lauren.

What are you looking for in a boyfriend?

I'm looking for someone who is sincere and who will listen to me. I go for quiet guys because I like to do a lot of talking. Someone good-looking — but that's not major. Just basically nice.

Do you have a best friend?

The closest of my friends is like Patty [Lauren's best friend in *Square Pegs*]. We're both offbeat. We don't fit in with the kids we go to school with. We live in Beverly Hills now, but we're both from out of town.

When did you decide you wanted to become an actress?

When I was eight years old, I saw Kristy McNichol in *Apple's Way*. I thought, "Gee, that looks like fun, and she has that good-looking brother, Vince Van Patten. I want to do that!" Then I started watching her in *Family*. I loved her character in that show. I thought she was great and I just kept on watching her. She's been my idol since I was eight years old. I guess it was her acting that really inspired me.

But even before then, I used to lock my relatives in the bedroom and do shows for them. I've always been an entertainer. I'd make up shows with my little brother. I'd direct and produce and stage my own productions in the house. We'd parody commercials and TV shows, and we'd have a lot of fun.

Where are you from?

I was born in Brooklyn and raised in Forest Hills, so I'm a transplanted New Yorker living in Beverly Hills — which is not what it's cracked up to be! What can I tell you?

When my friends from New York ask me where I'm living and I say Beverly Hills, they say, "Ex-cuuuuuuuuse me!"

What has high school been like for you?

Well, it's weird. In Forest Hills, I never fitted in with the kids I went to school with. I was always different. I was a square peg because I knew where I wanted to be on Saturdays. I didn't want to be hanging out at the local mall. I wanted to be at acting school.

The kids I went to school with didn't understand. My good friends did, but the other kids couldn't understand how I could know what I wanted to do so early in life. I just knew.

I never wanted to fit in in New York. I wanted to fit in with the kids who *didn't* fit in. I wanted to be different. I marched to the beat of my own drum.

When I came out here, I was having an identity crisis because I couldn't find my crazy clothes and the same New York spots, and I didn't know where to go find them. When I started going to Beverly Hills [high school] full-time, which was in February, I felt a lot of peer pressure. The pressure at Beverly is so hard to overcome, and I didn't feel too terrific about myself when I walked into that school. In order to make friends there you have to have nice clothes, and so I started to dress like everyone else. But now that I have friends, I feel I can throw away all my nice clothes and start dressing crazy again.

After a while, I started to realize that the kids

who judge you on your appearance are not the kids I want to be friends with. And I've found my own crowd — my own clique. The out-kids again. The square pegs.

Do you have any hobbies?

I roller-skate. I like to do that. I'm going to try to do it every day for at least an hour because that's how I'm going to get exercise. In New York I took dance classes and went to acting school for four years, but I haven't had time for that here because I've been working so much and going to school.

I like to read, and write letters. I love listening to music. I play the flute. Oh, you know what I do? This is soooooooo embarrassing. I love talking on the phone!

I called a friend of mine at a quarter after twelve A.M. I couldn't fall asleep. I was listening to music and I was practically crying. I missed my friends from camp.

I called my friend Krispen, a very good friend of mine, a male friend — sometimes it's easier to talk to a guy — and we talked till five-thirty in the morning. He cheered me up in ten minutes, but the rest of the time we just kept talking. We talked about everything. I love talking on the phone. It's peaceful talking when it's quiet out.

All of a sudden it was five o'clock. He said, "I think the sun is rising." I said, "Oh, my gosh! We'd better get off the phone." The next day, I was like a zombie!

Doesn't it hurt your ear to talk on the phone that long?

No! I've had my own phone since I was eleven because my mom knew how much I needed it! I have this compulsion to talk all the time. I just got a new phone. The top is blue and the bottom white so it matches my room. I love it!

Do you have any long-term goals?

Yeah! There are lots of things that I want to do in this business, and then again, there are so many things I want to do *out* of this business! I'm determined to do ninety-nine percent of them if I can't do them all.

In acting, I want to do movies. I'm very interested in that. I really want to work with Kristy McNichol in a movie — a blockbuster hit. A *Star Wars*, *E.T.*, *Raiders of the Lost Ark.* Something like Steven Spielberg does.

And I'd like to do at least one role where I have love scenes on the beach.

With whom?

Oh, I don't know. I like so many young actors today! I couldn't tell you! Well, if Robert Redford were a little younger, maybe. Or Warren Beatty. I could go for Timothy Hutton. He's not too old. Even Doug McKeon. He's cute.

I have one real big ambition, besides performing at the White House. I definitely want to do something like Sylvester Stallone did. I want to produce, write, direct, and star in my own movie. Maybe I'll leave out producing. But I'd like to write and direct and act in a movie. My life story!

WE INTERRUPT THIS BOOK TO BRING YOU THESE IMPORTANT MESSAGES . . .

TV today offers more than ever. With special equipment, you can use your TV screen to play video games, figure out your budget, and watch your own home-made or store-bought movies. For a monthly fee, you can tune in to dozens of additional channels and see recently released movies, uncut and commercial-free. With two-way TV, you can shop and take classes through the tube!

In the following pages, you'll find out about all the new things you can do with your TV. So read on — and join the smart set!

GETTING HOOKED ON PAY AND PLAY TV

Cable TV gets a warm reception

The three networks send electronic signals for their TV shows to local stations through telephone wires. Then the local stations (called affiliates) send the signals through the air from their antenna to yours.

If there are mountains or tall buildings between your antenna and the affiliate's antenna, your picture will be poor. Cable TV started as a way to improve reception in areas that couldn't be reached clearly by broadcasting. The way it works is very simple.

The cable company puts up its own giant antenna that can receive the broadcast clearly. Then they send you the signal through wires — and a monthly bill through the mail.

Cable TV has been around since 1948 as a way to improve reception. In the fifties, cable subscribers numbered in the thousands. Now, twenty-three million Americans are hooked on cable TV. That's twenty-nine percent of all the homes that have television.

Obviously, improved reception is not the only reason people subscribe to cable TV. Cable offers more channels. Some of the channels are included in the cost of the basic cable service. You don't have to pay extra for them. A few of the basic channels that a cable company might offer are ESPN, an all-sports channel; MTV, a music channel; Nickelodeon, a children's channel; CBS, a cultural channel; there's even an all-weather channel.

In addition to the basic channels, cable subscribers can buy premium channels. These channels offer recently released movies, special sports events, and concerts. Home Box Office was the first company to offer this type of service. Now as many people watch HBO in a given night as watch the network shows! And you can bet your selector there are lots more pay channels coming up!

One interesting thing about cable TV is that it can be a two-way street. If talking back to your TV sounds too futuristic for you, you've got some catching up to do! Qube is no longer on ice! Qube, from Warner Communications, is a two-way cable system that's available in Pittsburgh, Pennsylvania, and Cincinnati and Columbus, Ohio.

The usual cable system sends information from the cable station to the viewer's home. Two-way does that *and* it sends information from the viewer's home back to the cable station. It's no surprise that two-way systems are very expensive to set up.

A Qube subscriber has an electronic box with thirty channels and five response buttons. After viewers are asked a question during a TV show, they press one of the response buttons. Responses go to a computer in the Qube studio, and the results appear on the viewer's TV screen.

Typically, Qube viewers may be asked to judge a talent contest or they may be asked opinions on political issues. Qube is also experimenting with other uses. They are beginning to offer burglar and fire alarm systems, shop-at-home services, and a cable classroom called Qube Campus.

A student of the Qube Campus can ask a teacher to speed up or slow down; and the Qube Campus can give exams, mark them, and keep report cards. If a Qube student has a question, he or she presses a button; the question is heard and answered, using telephones. Say good-bye to the boob tube!

The games TVs play

"You're crazy! Nobody will pay twenty-five cents to play a game without a long paddle."

That's what pinball manufacturers told Nolan Bushnell when he went to them with an idea for a coin-operated video game called Pong. Bushnell and his friends had gotten together in his garage and invented Pong. In Pong, two players bat a ball of light back and forth, as in a Ping-Pong game.

Since Bushnell couldn't sell the idea, he formed his own company, Atari. Pong appeared in 1972, and soon pinball players everywhere started turning on to it.

Pong was only the beginning. In 1977, Atari found a way to move these video games out of the arcade and into the living room with their Video Computer System (VCS). As everyone knows, this system hooks up to a TV set, which becomes the screen for the games. Then you plug in a controller and insert a game cartridge. The end result is that the biggest star of TV today may be the silicon chip. (The chip is what makes video games possible.)

Atari brings it home

More than a hundred game cartridges can be used with Atari VCS. Not only does Atari make cartridges for the VCS, but other companies, such as ActiVision and Imagic, also make cartridges that fit this system.

The large number of games is one reason for the success of Atari VCS. Another reason is that Atari offers home versions of the most popular coin-op games. Asteroids, Missile Command, Pac-Man, Galaxian, Space Invaders, and Defender are all available as Atari game cartridges.

One of the shortcomings of the Atari VCS is that the graphics aren't as detailed as the competition's. This isn't true of the new Atari 400 and Atari 800. The new Ataris have larger memories than the VCS, so the graphics are better and the games can be more complicated.

The Atari 400 and 800 are primarily personal computers — and they're priced that way. To turn the personal computer into a home video game, you have to buy the controllers separately. The bad news is that cartridges for the Atari VCS do not fit into the Atari 400 and 800. The good news is that Atari has done some pretty fancy stuff with the cartridges that have been made for the new computers. So far, Star Raiders, Missile Command, Basketball, Computer Chess, Super Breakout, 3-D Tic-Tac-Toe, Space Invaders, Pac-Man, and Asteroids are available. When you see them you'll agree — they're the most impressive home video games this side of the Zylon Empire!

Tuning in to Intellivision

The word among home video pros is this — for home versions of coin-op games, it's Atari; for exciting sports games, it's Intellivision.

In some ways, Intellivision is similar to Atari's Video Computer System. Attach a switch box to a color TV, plug in a couple of wires, pick up one of the hand controls, and you're set to play.

One major difference between the two systems is that Intellivision has a larger memory than Atari VCS. That's why Intellivision games look so much better — and that's why Intellivision sports games are really something else!

43

The Major League Baseball cartridge lets you control pitching, fielding, base running, and batting. With the NBA Basketball cartridge, players can pass, catch, jump, and dribble. The NFL Football game has one hundred eighty different plays for passing, running, tackling, and intercepting — and it even comes complete with crowd noises. As the man in the ad says, these video sports are as close to the real thing as possible.

Last licks

Coleco waited several years before they came out with their version of a home video game system. ColecoVision was worth the wait! ColecoVision has a large memory for great games and super graphics. It comes with a stick, a roller, and a key pad for variety.

Coleco has been busy buying up rights to produce home versions of coin-op hits such as Donkey-Kong, Turbo, Vanguard, and Phoenix. They've also added their own Venture, Ripcord, Lady Bug, and Mouse Trap to their lineup. The most exciting feature, though, is that you can use Atari VCS cartridges with it! It's home video heaven!

Play TV—are you game?

"The video game market is hyperspace hot!" says an ad for PlayCable. You can bet your Smart Bomb it is! Big bucks are being made off coin-operated games and home games alike. If the trend continues, PlayCable should be a surefire hit. PlayCable is TV's very first game station. Here's how it works.

Before you get PlayCable, you have to buy Mattel Electronics' Intellivision and subscribe to a cable service that offers PlayCable. When you sign up for it, you get an adapter that will pick up the games. Then you turn on the TV set and select a game, and the game appears on your screen.

Every month, PlayCable offers fifteen games from a pool of thirty-six. You can play any of the fifteen games at any time of the day and set the games for different levels of skill. The five favorite games of current PlayCable subscribers are Astrosmash, Baseball, Bowling, Space Armada, and Triple Action.

If the names of the games sound familiar, it's because these games are also sold as Intellivision cartridges. The advantage of PlayCable is that for a monthly fee that's cheaper than one game cartridge, you have fifteen games to choose from. It's a dream come true for armchair arcaders.

Home video vs. coin-op

Home versions of the popular arcade games such as Missile Command, Galaxian, Defender, Space Invaders, Pac-Man, and Asteroids are never exact duplicates of the originals. One reason is that the computer used in a home video system doesn't have as large a memory as the coin-op computer. Another reason is that the screens of coin-op games are usually vertical and the screen on your TV is horizontal. Also, the button and stick controllers are more accurate on coin-op versions.

Most games experts I talked to agreed that home video and coin-op are two different experiences. To find out for myself, I chose Pac-Man as my "guinea pig," and spent many hours and many quarters investigating how the home game differs from the arcade version. Here's what I learned.

Pac-Man, arcade-style

Pac-Man isn't a very pretty fellow, but we've grown accustomed to his face. He looks like a pie with a piece cut out. With a stick controller, you and Pac-Man try to clear a maze of two hundred forty small dots and four large dots. Pac-Man gets ten points for small dots and fifty points for large dots.

While he's munching on dots, Pac-Man must avoid four monsters, who are eager to do Pac-Man in and end the round. If the monsters are hot on his tail, Pac-Man may leave the board through a tunnel on one side of the maze and return on the other side. The monsters' eyes tell you when they're changing direction, which gives you and Pac-Man a break.

When Pac-Man eats one of the large dots (called energizers), the monsters (who are red, green, pink, and orange) turn blue. During their blue period, Pac-Man can try to catch the monsters for big points — two hundred for the first, four hundred for the second, eight hundred for the third, and sixteen hundred for the fourth. The trapped monsters briefly return to the monster pen in the center of the board, where they turn back to their original colors and then continue to chase Pac-Man.

You can also get a lot of points by eating one of the fruits, which flash on the board occasionally. They're called fruits, even though some of them aren't.

If Pac-Man eats all the dots on the board, you get a new one. You get three Pac-Men per game, and an extra if you get more than ten thousand points.

High-scoring Pac-Maniacs use patterns when they play. They find a path that lets them complete a board and then use the same path time after time.

Pac-Man at home

Scoring is very different in the home version of Pac-Man. Everything is worth less, so expect your home score to be about one-tenth less than your arcade score. The lingo is also different. In the home version, monsters are called ghosts, energizers are called power pills, and fruits are replaced with vitamins.

The first difference you'll notice in the home version is that Pac-Man isn't round. He's a bit jagged around the edge. He and the ghosts are paler.

Pac-Man gets fewer points for catching ghosts in the home version. The first ghost is worth twenty points, the second ghost is worth forty points, the third ghost is worth sixty points, and the fourth ghost is worth one hundred sixty points. The ghosts are more dangerous because their eyes don't tell you where they're going. Also, Pac-Man will shrivel up after the slightest brush with a ghost in this version, where he might still be safe in the other.

You'll notice that there are dashes — one hundred twenty-six of them — instead of dots in the maze. The dashes are worth one point and the power pills are worth five points.

The maze is also different. It is horizontal rather than vertical, and the exit tunnels are at the top and the bottom. There are more barriers that you have to move Pac-Man around. If you have a pattern for the arcade version, it won't work here. You have to develop a new one.

One problem with the home version is that the stick is harder to control, so it's harder to move Pac-Man around. That means you'll need more practice.

One of the great advantages of the home version is that you can control the speeds of Pac-Man and the ghost, and you can adjust the length of time the ghosts remain blue and vulnerable. If you give yourself a fast Pac-Man and slow ghosts, you'll rack up thousands of points. On the other hand, if you can clear a board with a slow Pac-Man and fast ghosts, you'll prove you're a Pac-Man pro!

Tips for Pac-Man players

The games experts I talked to said these tips will work for both the arcade and the home video versions of Pac-Man:

- Try to eat as many of the dots/dashes as you can before getting to the energizers/power pills. Of course, if you're in a jam, don't hesitate — energize!
- If the monsters/ghosts are hot on Pac-Man's trail, try escaping through a tunnel. *But* before you do this, make sure the opposite end of the tunnel is clear.
- If Pac-Man isn't being chased, you might want to wait around for more monsters/ghosts to come

closer before you eat an energizer/power pill. Then you can catch more monsters and get more points.

The final score

In my opinion, the home video games aren't quite as exciting to play as the coin-op ones. But think about this. You don't have to keep feeding a home game quarters, and when you're trying to learn a game, those quarters add up quickly. Also, when you have a home video system, you don't have to wait hours for your favorite game while the person in front of you is scoring in the billions.

SOME FACTS ABOUT LISA WHELCHEL'S LIFE!

She's extremely wealthy. She's spoiled rotten. She's a super snob. She's very, very, *very* vain. But her fans love her. Or at least they love to hate her. Who is she? She is the beautiful Blair on NBC's hit comedy series, *The Facts of Life*. Nineteen-year-old Lisa Whelchel plays Blair, and except for the part about being beautiful, Lisa is nothing at all like her character.

"Even though Blair and I are very different, it surprises me how easy it is to play her and how much I enjoy it," said Lisa. "I love the Blair character. She has so much depth to her," Lisa continued. "Despite her arrogance and conceit, she's saved by the fact that she doesn't realize she's this way at all."

To listen to Lisa and to watch her in action, it's hard to believe this Texas-born actress had ever been shy. But it was her shyness that actually got her into acting in the first place.

"To help me get over my shyness, my mother enrolled me in a drama class, and I really took to it," Lisa explained. "I started appearing in stage productions when I was seven."

The last Mouseketeer

By the time she was twelve, Lisa wanted to try out for bigger things. When she learned that they were holding auditions in California for *The New Mickey Mouse Club*, she wanted to be one of the Mouseketeers. So she talked her mother into flying to Los Angeles with her so she could audition. By the time Lisa auditioned, thousands of kids had already been seen. There was only one Mouseketeer spot left.

As it turned out, Lisa got that spot. After four *long* weeks of waiting back home in Fort Worth, Texas, Lisa received the all-important telephone call telling her she had been chosen as the last Mouseketeer! She was thrilled. But there was one big problem. How was she going to live in Texas and work in California?

Her family solved that problem for her. "It wasn't easy," Lisa recalled. "But my family knew that acting was what I wanted to do with my life, and they knew I wanted to do it while I was young. So while I was working, either my mother or my grandmother would come from Texas to live with me."

Lisa missed her family and friends and Fort Worth terribly. But when *The New Mickey Mouse Club* ended after the first year on TV, did she happily return home to live? Not on your life! Lisa's love of acting won out over her love of Fort Worth. For five years, her mom and her grandmother traded off staying with her while Lisa had guest roles in several TV shows and appeared in two movies. She didn't get every role she tried out for, but she did leave a lasting impression.

The matter of Facts

When *The Facts of Life* was being cast, one TV executive remembered her from a previous audition. Lisa was contacted. She tested for the role of Blair and has played Blair ever since. That was three years ago. Since then the show has grown in popularity and in maturity. The show often deals with problems that teens really have. Even though the scripts are funny, they also have some serious points.

Facts has had episodes dealing with dating, marriage, drinking, and drugs. Actress/comedian Geri Jewell, who has cerebral palsy, brings attention to some of the problems faced by the handicapped when she makes occasional appearances as Blair's cousin.

"It happens to be a quality show that people of all ages can enjoy," Lisa said.

In the three years that they've been together, Lisa, Kim, and co-stars Nancy (Jo) McKeon, and Mindy (Natalie) Cohn have grown very close. "We work well together because we genuinely like each other," says Lisa. "We always work eight hours. On Mondays we start at nine in the morning. On Tuesdays not until eleven-thirty, because we tape until nine P.M. On Thursdays we start at nine-thirty."

Outside of the cast, Lisa said she knows "just about every young person in the business, because of the parties and different functions we all attend, but I'm not really best friends with any of them."

Lisa still keeps in touch with friends back in Fort Worth. "My friends think it's great that I'm on *Facts*. It hasn't changed our relationships, except I don't get to see them as much," Lisa said. She visits Fort Worth at least once a month.

On her own

Lisa has been living on her own in California since she was seventeen years old. "When I turned seventeen it was just easier for me to live alone. I didn't have to go to school anymore, and at that time I'd basically been on my own long enough to handle it."

Lisa graduated from high school—with honors—when she was sixteen. While her castmates are doing schoolwork (for at least three hours a day), Lisa has time to play racquetball or take an exercise class. Exercising helps her watch her weight.

"I've had a problem with my weight all my life," Lisa said. As far as she is concerned, what a person is like on the inside is more important than what a person is like on the outside. But since Blair is *very* particular about her outward appearance, Lisa has to be that way, too—at least for the TV screen. That means staying trim, which is not always so easy for Lisa because she loves to eat.

When asked about the best part of the day on the set, she quickly replied, "Lunch! Yes, one o'clock when we all go to lunch! We all have a good time going someplace different every day."

Going out to lunch can present yet another problem for Lisa. It's no secret that Blair loves getting noticed. Well, Lisa doesn't. She dislikes being recognized in public. Though she is friendly to her fans and signs autographs, she says, "I'm not really comfortable when I get a lot of attention."

Lisa doesn't think of herself as being a star. She doesn't even watch herself on television. But she does tape *Facts* regularly. She explained, "I want to show it to my kids someday!"

TV YESTERDAY

Tune In To 1960

Here's what you would have seen if you had turned on your TV set any evening in 1960!

	ABC	CBS	NBC
Sunday			
7:00	Walt Disney Presents	Lassie	Shirley Temple's Storybook
7:30	Maverick	Dennis the Menace	
8:00		Ed Sullivan Show	National Velvet
8:30	The Lawman		Tab Hunter Show
9:00	The Rebel	G.E. Theater	Dinah Shore Chevy Show
9:30	The Islanders	Jack Benny Show	
10:00		Candid Camera	Loretta Young Show
10:30	Walter Winchell Show	What's My Line?	This Is Your Life

Dennis the Menace

	ABC	**CBS**	**NBC**
Monday			
7:30	Cheyenne	To Tell the Truth	Riverboat
8:00		Pete & Gladys	
8:30	Surfside Six	Bringing Up Buddy	Tales of Wells Fargo
9:00		Danny Thomas Show	Klondike
9:30	Adventures in Paradise	Andy Griffith Show	Dante
10:00		Hennessey	Barbara Stanwyck Show
10:30	Peter Gunn	Presidential Countdown	Jackpot Bowling
Tuesday			
7:30	Bugs Bunny Show		Laramie
8:00	The Rifleman	Father Knows Best	
8:30	Wyatt Earp	Dobie Gillis	Alfred Hitchcock Presents
9:00	Stagecoach West	Tom Ewell Show	Thriller
9:30		Red Skelton Show	
10:00	Alcoa Presents	Gary Moore Show	
Wednesday			
7:30	Hong Kong	Aquanauts	Wagon Train
8:30	Ozzie & Harriet	Wanted: Dead or Alive	Price Is Right
9:00	Hawaiian Eye	My Sister Eileen	Perry Como's Kraft Music Hall
9:30		I've Got a Secret	
10:00	Naked City	Armstrong Circle Theatre	Peter Loves Mary

	ABC	**CBS**	**NBC**
Thursday			
7:30	Guestward Ho!	The Witness	The Outlaws
8:00	Donna Reed Show		
8:30	Real McCoys	Zane Grey Theatre	Bat Masterson
9:00	My Three Sons	Angel	Bachelor Father
9:30	The Untouchables	Peck's Bad Girl	Ford Show
10:00		Person to Person	Groucho Show
10:30	Take a Good Look	DuPont Show	
Friday			
7:30	Matty's Funday Funnies	Rawhide	Dan Raven
8:00	Harrigan & Son		
8:30	The Flintstones	Route 66	The Westerner
9:00	77 Sunset Strip		Bell Telephone Hour
9:30		Mr. Garlund	
10:00	The Detectives	Twilight Zone	Michael Shayne
10:30	Law & Mr. Jones	Eyewitness to History	
Saturday			
7:30	Roaring Twenties	Perry Mason	Bonanza
8:30	Leave It to Beaver	Checkmate	Tall Man
9:00	Lawrence Welk Show		The Deputy
9:30		Have Gun Will Travel	Nation's Future
10:00	Fight of the Week	Gunsmoke	

HOW FAME CAME TO LEE CURRERI

I met Lee Curreri at a theater in Los Angeles, where the NBC series, *Fame*, was being filmed. Lee and I sat in the green room while Erica Gimpel, who plays Coco, and some other dancers were rehearsing on stage. Lee wasn't needed in this scene, so he took some time out to talk to us.

Music is the message

Lee grew up just north of New York City in Yonkers. Although neither of his parents was musical, they soon got the message that Lee was.

"Wherever there was a keyboard, I would start plunking," he said. "And then when I was six and a half, my parents had me go to a private teacher to take piano lessons."

By the time Lee was in junior high school, he decided that he wanted to become a professional musician.

"My parents were totally against it," Lee told me. "They said, 'We gave you music lessons as a hobby.

We didn't mean for you to take it seriously.' But it was too late. I had already taken it seriously."

In the TV version of the High School for Performing Arts, it isn't uncommon for Lee's character, Bruno, to be among fellow students pirouetting down the halls, jamming in the cafeteria, and bursting into song during study hall. High school wasn't quite the same for Lee himself, who attended Fordham Prep High School in New York. Fordham Prep is an all-boys' school, taught by Jesuit priests. The emphasis there is *not* on the performing arts.

"The band was the worst in the world," Lee said. He felt that the band actually sounded better when they deliberately made mistakes! At least, that way the band sounded funny rather than just plain bad.

"In our senior year, we had a lot of independent classes," Lee explained. "We would just report to a teacher once a term without having to go to classes. Usually those free days were spent sitting in the English center writing parodies and skits and doing imitations. We spent a lot of time with the literary magazine. I was the editor, so that took up more of my time and energy than any of the schoolwork."

Of course, another thing that took up Lee's time and energy was music. Lee, who was the musical director for the Fordham Prep plays, attended the Manhattan School of Music on Saturdays.

Because he skipped two years of grammar school, Lee was only fifteen when he graduated from high school. He then attended Mannes College of Music, where he studied composition for a year. After that he worked as a free-lance arranger for singers and played piano for improvisational comedy groups. Lee's ambition had been to become a successful composer and arranger, but then his career took a sudden turn toward Hollywood.

Playing for reel

Fame came to Lee in 1979, when the producers of the movie were looking for someone to play the role of Bruno. They needed someone who could act, play the piano, and look Italian.

A teacher at the Manhattan School of Music recommended Lee, who fit the bill and got the part. When the TV pilot was produced for NBC, the president of the network demanded, "Get me the kid who played the piano."

"I studied acting when I was ten," Lee said, "but when I had to make a living, I concentrated on music. Then the movie came along, and all of a sudden I was called to play a musician. I got the part and it whetted my appetite for acting again. I was definitely not expecting it and most definitely not looking for it!"

One of the best things about working on *Fame* is that Lee gets to write songs for the show. He's also writing a script.

"Conversation is very musical," he explained. "There's a definite rhythm to the way people talk. I have a good ear for it, so I can write dialogue. The plot is the hardest thing. The dialogue is easy."

Fame has become a creative outlet for Lee as an actor, a composer, and a writer. That's a great stroke

of luck for him. One result of this good fortune is that his parents have changed their tune about Lee's chosen career. "They love it," he said. "They're schoolteachers and they teach kids who watch the show. They're getting more mileage out of it than I am!"

RIGHT AT HOME WITH STEPHEN COLLINS

Stephen Collins has just moved into a new apartment. It is in a beautiful, Spanish-style building with sunny courtyards and shady paths.

"It's the first and only apartment that I looked at," Stephen said. "It's not big in terms of square feet, but it has an open, wonderful, sunny feeling to it. It's the first place I've ever lived where I'm eager to have people come over!"

When we asked to interview the star of *Tales of the Gold Monkey*, Stephen Collins suggested — where else? — his new apartment! So make yourself comfortable, and join me for our question-and-answer session . . .

What is the gold monkey?

There's a legend that a huge gold idol was built to commemorate a monkey who helped some people find their way through the South Pacific islands. This monkey pointed toward land when the people were lost — they followed the monkey and found the land. When they got there, the monkey died, so they built the idol. Nobody really knows whether the story is true or not.

What is your character, Jake Cutter, all about?

He was a baseball player whose arm went bad on him. He couldn't play baseball anymore, so he turned to his other love, which was flying.

He's definitely an old-fashioned, 1930s-type movie hero. He doesn't think of himself as a hero at all, as most heroes don't. Those characters tend to act definitely and quickly. They don't like to sit around and think about things. They *do* things. It's really fun to put on that uniform and become this guy who does wonderful things all the time.

Why did you decide to do Tales of the Gold Monkey?

I'd been offered about five or six other pilots for this season, all of which had two-dimensional and straightforward characters — earnest young doctors or flashy young detectives.

If I was going to give myself over to the schedule of doing a series, I wanted it to be something I really loved. There are too many other things to do. When I read *Gold Monkey*, I thought, "Here it is!" I could be happy getting up at six-thirty in the morning every day, day after day, and going in to work on it!

There was something about this script that really got me. The combination of adventure and humor and romance was wonderful. When I read the *Gold Monkey* pilot script, I couldn't believe it was for television. It was so good! It was so well written!

How does an actor know if a script is going to make a good TV series?

There's just something in the mind that says, "Yes, this is it!" One actor might look at a script and say that, but another actor might look at the same script and not feel that way about it. It may not click with the things that are important at that moment to that person.

I think it's mostly intuitive. Children have great intuition. Adults unlearn their intuition. Adults start trusting their intellect more than their gut. I think it's a tremendous mistake. The intellect is very important, but that first stab of feeling that says yes or no to something is never wrong!

That's why I admire kids. Kids just know what they want to do!

What were you like when you were a kid?

I had to wear thick glasses and heavy braces, and I hated it. I was like the ugly duckling. It was a very tough time. No matter how advantaged I was otherwise — I mean, I had a very lovely background in terms of being comfortable — I had a lot of turbulence going on inside.

I was painfully shy. I was afraid of any kind of open demonstration of anything. I was not very competitive. I was fearful of getting up in front of my peers, my friends, and looking like a jerk. As a result, I often didn't try things that I wanted to do very badly. I was a very *good* kid. I mean, I got good grades. But I was full of a lot of pain and a lot of confusion.

What kinds of things were you afraid to do?

Well, simple things. Sports, for instance. For years I wanted to play in the Little League, but I always found an excuse not to. There were two days of tryouts, and I just couldn't do it, so I never played in Little League. I didn't want to compete. I talked myself into thinking that the reason I wasn't doing it was that my family went away during the end of the season. But they would have let me play on the team and then leave the last couple of weeks.

—

Did you dream of becoming a baseball player?

I wanted to be a baseball player badly when I was a kid, but fate or nature or whatever sort of took care of it for me. I'm almost blind in one eye. I was born that way. I was a good fielder, but I couldn't hit a ball. So it was not really a choice that I had to make.

One of the fun parts about being an actor is that you can make your fantasies come alive. In *Gold Monkey,* the whole baseball thing is mine. It's a little sidelight we put into the character, just for fun for me. Jake got a lot farther along in his career than I did, but he was thwarted, too!

When you were a kid, did you dream of becoming an actor?

I wanted to act from the time I was very small. I wanted to so badly that I never told anybody. It was just my secret. I was terribly worried as the years went on that I wouldn't try. Even when I went off to college, I had talked myself into thinking that I'd probably be a lawyer.

What brought you out of your shyness?

When I was in high school, a friend of mine talked me into joining his band. He said, "I'll teach you how to play bass guitar." He was going to be the lead singer, so I would just be in the background. I could never have been the lead singer at that point!

Being in the band taught me that there was nothing to be afraid of. If you are having a good time at something you want to do, just go ahead and do it. Don't worry about whether people are going to laugh at you.

The year that I started playing in the band was also when I first acted in a play at high school. Somehow I had also mustered up the courage to try out for plays. It went wonderfully. I was suddenly thought of as someone who could act. And of course, as soon as I was thought of as someone who could act, it was easy for me to audition for plays.

Once I have a foot in the door, I'm fine. But until people thought of me as someone who could act, before I played in the band, before I got into plays, it just killed me inside not to be part of it. I just didn't know how to break through. The band was a real breakthrough for me.

What do you do for fun?

I act. Acting is really fun. The whole reason I got into this was for fun.

I play a little softball, although not as much as I'd like to anymore. I love to go to ball games. There's something timeless about the ball park. The fact that baseball isn't played to a clock is very, very relaxing.

It's funny. Because my work keeps me so busy, I like nothing better than a day when I have to do

some laundry or go to the store to buy some food. Housework, dumb as it sounds, is something you can point to and know you've done it right. You can do the dishes and they're done. It's a very small sense of accomplishment, but it's very clear. I appreciate those things more and more as other things in life get more complicated.

TV YESTERDAY

Tune In To 1970

Here's what you would have seen if you had turned on your TV set any evening in 1970!

	ABC	CBS	NBC
Sunday			
7:00	Young Rebels	Lassie	Wild Kingdom
7:30		Hogan's Heroes	Wonderful World of Disney
8:00	The F.B.I.	Ed Sullivan Show	
8:30			Bill Cosby Show
9:00	Sunday Night Movie	Glen Campbell Hour	Bonanza
10:00		Tim Conway Comedy Hour	Bold Ones
Monday			
7:30	Young Lawyers	Gunsmoke	Red Skelton Show
8:00			Rowan & Martin's Laugh-In
8:30	Silent Force	Here's Lucy	
9:00	Monday Night Football	Mayberry R.F.D.	Monday Night Movie
9:30		Doris Day Show	
10:00		Carol Burnett Show	

	ABC	**CBS**	**NBC**
Tuesday			
7:30	Mod Squad	Beverly Hillbillies	Don Knotts Show
8:00		Green Acres	
8:30	Movie of the Week	Hee Haw	Julia
9:00			Tuesday Night Movie
9:30		To Rome with Love	
10:00	Marcus Welby, M.D.	60 Minutes	
Wednesday			
7:30	Courtship of Eddie's Father	Storefront Lawyers	Men from Shiloh
8:00	Make Room for Grandaddy		
8:30	Room 222	Governor & J.J.	
9:00	Johnny Cash Show	Medical Center	Kraft Music Hall
10:00	Dan August	Hawaii Five-O	Four in One
Thursday			
7:30	Matt Lincoln	Family Affair	Flip Wilson Show
8:00		Jim Nabors Hour	
8:30	Bewitched		Ironside
9:00	Barefoot in the Park	Thursday Night Movie	
9:30	The Odd Couple		Nancy
10:00	The Immortal		Dean Martin Show
Friday			
7:30	Brady Bunch	The Interns	High Chaparral
8:00	Nanny & the Professor		
8:30	Partridge Family	The Headmaster	Name of the Game

The Partridge Family

	ABC	CBS	NBC
Friday			
:00	That Girl	Friday Night Movie	
:30	Love, American Style		
0:00	This Is Tom Jones		Bracken's World
Saturday			
:30	Let's Make a Deal	Mission: Impossible	Andy Williams Show
:00	Newlywed Game		
:30	Lawrence Welk Show	My Three Sons	Adam 12
:00		Arnie	Saturday Night Movie
:30	Most Deadly Game	Mary Tyler Moore Show	
0:00		Mannix	

KATHY MAISNIK—A STARSTRUCK STAR!

What's it like to suddenly be walking among all the television stars you watch and admire and adore? That's just what happened to Kathy Maisnik when she became the star of *Star of the Family!*

Like Jenny Lee Krebs, Kathy Maisnik is a young performer who's just starting out. Jenny Lee is the aspiring country-pop singer who is the main character in ABC-TV's *Star of the Family.* Kathy Maisnik is the actress who plays that character. *Star of the Family* is Kathy's very first professional job.

Her family and friends are all thrilled about Kathy's success. Some have advice and some have requests. Said Kathy, "My friend Amy told me, 'Look, are you ever going to meet Scott Baio? Because I really want his autograph!' "

When I talked to Kathy in a Hollywood restaurant, she was absolutely bursting with excitement about her new life! "It's so exciting for me to see all the famous people!" Kathy exclaimed. "I'm in awe of them. I met Scott Baio at a press conference! I met

Erin Moran and Pat Benetar one night, and it was overwhelming to me!"

Kathy, like the character she plays, has wanted to be in show business ever since she can remember. "I didn't take private lessons," she said. "I just did it in school—any little plays that would come out.

"I would work really hard when I got a part," she explained. "I took it very seriously."

Kathy's parents took her seriously, too. "My parents are really supportive," she told us. "When I'd have an audition, I'd take the script home and ask my mom to read it with me. She'd be really good. We'd sit down for hours!"

After she finished school, Kathy studied musical theater at the Musical Theatre Workshop in Los Angeles. "For three months, five nights a week, from about six to midnight, all we did was sing, dance, and act!" Now all of Kathy's hard work and seriousness have paid off!

Getting a foot in the door

Security is tight at the studios where television shows are produced. In order to get in, you have to be working on a show or you need special permission from someone in authority. Once in a very great while, people manage to get through.

"They had a *Happy Days* anniversary party a while back, and my friend and I snuck in. We got in with my cousin, who was a writer for the show. We got there late. I guess by the time we got there, they didn't care about who was coming in and going out."

Kathy didn't get to meet Scott Baio or Henry Winkler or Erin Moran or any of the rest of the cast, as she had hoped, but she did get to meet the casting director. It would have made a good story if the *Happy Days* casting director had immediately offered her a role on the show, but he didn't. Kathy and her friend had fun just the same.

When the producers of *Star of the Family* were looking for someone to play Jennie Lee, they sent out the usual call to agents.

"My agent sent me out originally. I was brand-new at it. I read a little bit and they asked me what I had done. I said, 'Well, I performed at Alhambra High School.' Not the most impressive credits. They didn't call me back."

The producers couldn't find anyone through the agents, so they called the Musical Theatre Workshop. The director of the school recommended Kathy, who was still studying there, and she went back for another audition.

"I went through four more interviews," Kathy explained. "Then I came home one day, and it was on my answering machine! I was very excited! I stood there and I screamed! No one was home, so there was no one I could tell. I just stood there. I couldn't believe it. I couldn't believe I could actually go on a TV lot and not have to sneak in!"

Playing the star

"The part of Jenny is really fun. I think Jenny's just like me. I really do," Kathy said. "Jenny's father is a fireman. He worries about what she's going to get into and who she's going to get involved with. Jenny's relationship with her father is very important, and she doesn't like to do things without his approval.

"My father's not a fireman, but my father's protective. He wants to know what I'm doing. I'm very close with my father." Kathy added, "And I'm beginning—just as Jenny is!"

Unlike Jenny's father, who isn't happy about his daughter's career, Kathy's father is bursting with pride.

"When I first did the pilot, he said, 'Don't tell anyone. What if it doesn't go? Don't even tell your friends!' Then I went to the store the next day, and everyone had heard about the show! My father had told everyone!"

But what about her friend, Amy? Did she ever get Scott Baio's autograph?

No, she's still waiting. Kathy explained: "When I saw him at the press conference, I couldn't say to him, 'My friend Amy wants your autograph'!"

But Amy shouldn't worry about it. Kathy will have lots more chances now!

THE COMMERCIAL SUCCESS OF TOM SELLECK

"I wake up and wonder what I'm doing," said Tom Selleck. "How did all this happen? I look in the mirror and I don't even know who that guy is!"

Maybe the face isn't familiar to Tom, but millions of other people recognize it! For sixteen years, we've been seeing Tom's face on billboards, in magazine ads, on TV commercials, and now in *Magnum, P.I.!*

Tom broke into show business in 1967. Although he bombed in his first appearance, it turned out for the best. Tom appeared as a contestant on *The Dating Game*. He was among three men who were hidden from a woman who asked them questions and then picked one as her date. The bad news: Tom was on twice and he lost both times! The good news: A talent scout from Twentieth Century-Fox

saw Tom on the show, and the studio offered him a contract. More bad news: Fox suddenly canceled its entire talent program!

Commercial break

It may have been the end of the talent program, but it wasn't the end of Tom. His theater arts teacher told Tom to try making TV commercials. That way Tom could earn some money while he was studying to become an actor.

In Tom's first commercial, he was cast as a basketball player whose final shot won the game. Since he played basketball all through high school and college, making the shot was the easy part. The hard part came when the team was celebrating in the usual sweaty locker room and chugg-a-lugging sodas. Tom just couldn't get the scene right. By the time he was finished, Tom had chugged down three quarts of the stuff!

Tom thinks that commercials are the B movies of our time—a good training ground for actors before they move on to other things. Tom knows a few things about commercials. He's made about fifty of them.

Tom also appeared in many print ads, where he feels he wasn't always treated justly. In 1975, Tom posed for a billboard ad that appeared all over the country for four years. The company paid Tom eight hundred fifty dollars but spent millions buying the advertising space. That didn't seem fair to Tom, and he felt ripped off.

Tom found that many people think that actors who model try to get by on their looks alone and can't act. That attitude made it hard for him to be taken seriously as an actor. Tom had been acting for thirteen years before *Magnum, P.I.* made him an "overnight" success!

Case closed

Tom spent a year and a half in a soap opera, *The Young and the Restless*. He also appeared as a guest on several TV dramas. His big break came when he appeared on *The Rockford Files*.

Tom was cast as a rich, flashy, egotistical private eye who drove Jim Rockford crazy. Rockford had to do all the dirty and dangerous work to solve a case, and then Tom's character would rush in and take all the credit. The audience really liked the character, so he appeared in a few more episodes. Then CBS decided Tom should have his own series.

The first time Tom got a script for *Magnum, P.I.* he rejected it. Magnum was supposed to be a James Bond-type hero who solved every case and got every girl. Tom hated it. He wanted to be cast as a guy who won a few and lost a few. Luckily, the network and the producers went along with Tom. His instincts proved to be right, because *Magnum, P.I.* is a hit!

Tom hopes that *Magnum, P.I.* will have a long and healthy run. "I know that seven years in the same role seems like an awfully long time," he said, "but the bottom line is that I've been trying for years to get regular work, and now that I've got it, I'm not going to give it up!"

PHILIP McKEON— JUST YOUR NORMAL, AVERAGE, EVERDAY TV STAR!

Eighteen-year-old Philip McKeon has been playing Tommy in *Alice* for the past seven years. In spite of that, Philip said, "I've had a very normal life. I think I really have. I didn't get much special treatment because I grew up on television. It didn't make much of a difference."

Philip started working on *Alice* when he was eleven. He's had an audience throughout his adolescence.

"I never really thought about it as growing up in front of millions of people," Philip told us, "because I never see the millions of people I'm growing up in front of!"

Philip began his show business career when he was four years old. It was actually Philip's younger sister who paved the way for him. His sister is *Facts of Life* star Nancy McKeon.

"My sister started working, and I got into it after her," Philip said. "Nance started when she was two. It was the idea of a friend of my dad's. He said, 'Why don't you take Nancy on this call?' My dad really didn't want to, but he figured if she got it, she could put some money away for college. She got it and she got more and more and more. We just got into it that way."

Philip was working in a Broadway play when he was called to audition for the role of Tommy in *Alice*.

"I tried out about three times. A month later, I got a call to come out here [Los Angeles] to take a screen test—and I got it."

Surprisingly, Philip wasn't at all nervous about his audition. "No," he said, "I had been on so many calls I didn't even think about it. I didn't know the impact it would have until I got it!"

Philip doesn't live here anymore

Getting the part in *Alice* meant that Philip would have to move from Forest Hills, New York, to Los Angeles.

"I like it in New York," Philip told us. "That's always home. When I go back, I feel as if I'm going home. My whole family is back there—all my cousins and aunts and uncles."

Even though it was hard to leave friends and family behind in New York, Philip found it easy to make new friends in California.

"I met a lot of kids through the business," he explained. "It isn't hard to make friends because you come in contact with a lot of people."

There weren't any other kids working on *Alice*, but that didn't bother Philip at all. He said, "Being the only kid was fun because I got more attention. I was the only kid there for them to help out, so I got a lot of really good advice. If there had been more kids, it would have been spread around and shared more."

Philip never received any formal acting lessons. He has learned most of what he knows about acting by working with the director on *Alice*.

Philip explained the difference between children who act and adults who act. "Young kids aren't caught up in thinking about methods. They don't have to think about how this guy says you should do this and that guy says you should do that and 'I have to have motivation and inspiration.' They don't think about that. They don't clog their minds. They just get out there and do it.

"I don't think you can do that all your life," Phil added. "As you get older, you have to find some reason behind what you're doing."

Phil's attitude about acting has changed a bit over the years. "I take it more seriously now," he said. "It's not a big joke and a big game. Well, maybe a big game, but not a big joke. I think I've gotten better."

Sibling rivalry?

What's it like to live under the same roof as someone who has a show on another network? Do Philip and Nancy McKeon argue the way other brothers and sisters do?

"Not that much," Philip explained, "because we haven't seen each other much lately. I think all the fighting comes from being together all the time, and we're never together that much."

It was different when they were younger. "We fought a lot," Phil said, "just about as much as any other brother and sister. We fought over everything.

"What usually happened was that we'd be playfighting, and then all of a sudden someone would get hit hard, and then he would go after the other one—and there would be a fight!

"But we always covered up for each other. When one of our parents walked into the room, we'd smile and pretend nothing was happening. But we fought about a lot of stuff."

In spite of the play-fights and the arguments over what to watch on TV, Phil has a very high opinion of his sister.

"Nance is a very, very, very hard worker," he boasted. "She's a great actress!"

Phil and Nancy live in a house in Studio City with their parents, a dog, and a cat. Phil told us he has absolutely no desire to move out on his own.

"It's good living at home," he explained. "You don't get lonely and you always have your dinner cooked!"

BEHIND THE SCENES OF BRING 'EM BACK ALIVE

What is it really like to be an actor? We read all about actors' social lives, their childhoods, their families, and their dreams. But what do we know about the time they spend when they're really being actors—when they're acting? The only way to find that out would be to visit a set. And that's what I did!

Frank Buck was a legendary wild animal collector. He gained worldwide fame for trapping animals in Asian jungles and bringing 'em back alive to zoos and circuses. CBS-TV's *Bring 'Em Back Alive* is loosely based on the life of Frank Buck. Luckily, I didn't have to travel to any jungles to track down the show's cast and crew. In fact, I found them filming in Burbank, California.

Most of *Bring 'Em Back Alive* is filmed on a soundstage. A soundstage is an incredible place.

It's a long, low, windowless building where set decorators, propmasters, and carpenters can recreate any time or place. They can even control the weather!

Building Number 24 is one of the two soundstages where *Bring 'Em Back Alive* is filmed. The whole building is one giant room. In one part of the room, a small house stands on concrete blocks.

That's Frank Buck's jungle home. Next to that, jungle trees line part of the wall. A large tent is set up in front of the trees. Actually, it's only half a tent. One side of the tent is left off so that the cameras can catch the action.

Lights, camera, action!

The day I watched the filming, Ron O'Neal, who plays H.H. in the show, was tied up inside the tent. Ron was very hot while he was standing under the lights, but a makeup woman had to spray his face with water so he would look even more sweaty on film.

A buzzer went off and a small red light went on by the door. All activity stopped. Everyone on the soundstage froze. Only the assistant director spoke.

"Places, please," he said. "Quiet, please. And roll, please."

A man shut a clapboard in front of the camera. "Action!"

The camera was rolling. A sound man kept a microphone directly over Ron's head as the actor delivered his lines, and someone else followed the script to make sure he didn't leave anything out.

"I say, what time do you people serve dinner?" H.H. asked. "I'm absolutely ravenous." There was a pause, and then, "Well, don't look so surprised, professor. I've never been tortured before. I had no idea it could give one such an appetite."

The scene was repeated over and over and over again. When it was finally done to the director's satisfaction, it has to be done over again! This time in close-up.

The camera lens had to be changed, the lights had to be set up again, and the camera had to be focused again. Ron's hands were untied, and the actor got away as quickly as he could. It was hot under those lights. He needed a break!

Stand-ins took the actors' places as the lights were set up and the camera was focused. Stand-ins are also called the second team. Actors are called the first team.

"It's a grueling job," said John Zee, one of the first team. "You're like a human piece of furniture."

I could see he was right. Being an actor didn't seem quite as glamorous as I had imagined. The actors who are in a scene have to stand under hot lights while they repeat the same lines again and again and again. The actors who aren't in the scene have to sit around and be quiet. It gets pretty boring.

"Television is a technical medium," John explained. "Most of the time is taken in setting things up. The actual shooting time is very short."

It takes seven days to film a one-hour episode of *Bring 'Em Back Alive*. Although everybody has Saturdays and Sundays off, it's not unusual for actors to work a twelve-hour day.

The buzzer went off again.

"First team, places," the assistant director shouted. "Starting positions."

"All the actors—keep your energy up," the director added. The actors had already put in a ten-hour day.

"I never realized how patient actors had to be," I whispered to John.

"We're very well paid for what we do," he replied.

Bruce Boxleitner, who plays the heroic Frank Buck, seemed to be taking it all in stride. In fact, he looked as if he were having fun. "I love it. I'm able to be Errol Flynn, John Wayne, and Clark Gable all in one role. It's like being in all my favorite movies at once!"

TV YESTERDAY

Tune In To 1980

How many of these shows are still around?

	ABC	CBS	NBC
Sunday			
8:00	Charlie's Angels	Archie Bunker's Place	CHiPs
8:30		One Day at a Time	
9:00	Sunday Night Movie	Alice	The Big Event
9:30		The Jeffersons	
10:00		Trapper John, M.D.	

	ABC	**CBS**	**NBC**
Monday			
8:00	That's Incredible	Flo	Little House on the Prairie
8:30		Ladies' Man	
9:00	Monday Night Football	M*A*S*H	Monday Night Movie
9:30		House Calls	
10:00		Lou Grant	
Tuesday			
8:00	Happy Days	White Shadow	Sheriff Lobo
8:30	Laverne & Shirley		
9:00	Three's Company	Tuesday Night Movie	B.J. & the Bear
9:30	Too Close for Comfort		
10:00	Hart to Hart		Steve Allen Comedy Hour
Wednesday			
8:00	Eight Is Enough	Enos	Real People
9:00	Taxi	Wednesday Night Movie	Diff'rent Strokes
9:30	Soap		Facts of Life
10:00	Vegas		Quincy
Thursday			
8:00	Mork & Mindy	The Waltons	Games People Play
8:30	Bosom Buddies		
9:00	Barney Miller	Magnum, P.I.	Thursday Night Movie
10:00	20/20	Knot's Landing	

	ABC	**CBS**	**NBC**
Friday			
8:00	Benson	Incredible Hulk	Marie
8:30	I'm a Big Girl Now		
9:00	Friday Night Movie	Dukes of Hazzard	Speak Up Americ
10:00		Dallas	NBC Magazine
Saturday			
8:00	Breaking Away	WKRP in Cincinnati	Barbara Mandrel
8:30		Tim Conway Show	
9:00	Love Boat	Freebie and the Bean	Walking Tall
10:00	Fantasy Island	Secrets of Midland Heights	Hill Street Blues

WE'RE NUMBER 1!

Here is a list of the top-rated TV shows for the last 30 years as measured by the A.C. Nielsen Company. These shows had the largest audiences all year.

1951 — Texaco Star Theater: a comedy-variety show starring Milton Berle

1952 — Arthur Godfrey's Talent Scouts: where the audience rated hopeful amateurs

1953 — I Love Lucy: a zany situation comedy starring Lucille Ball

1954 — I Love Lucy

1955 — I Love Lucy

1956—The $64,000 Question: a quiz show where ordinary people got the chance to win big money

1957—I Love Lucy

1958—Gunsmoke: a Western that ran for twenty years with the same star, James Arness

1959—Gunsmoke

1960—Gunsmoke

1961—Gunsmoke

1962—Wagon Train: a Western about pioneers making their way out west

1963—The Beverly Hillbillies: a sitcom about hillbillies who struck it rich and moved to Beverly Hills

1964—The Beverly Hillbillies

1965—Bonanza: a Western about a wealthy rancher and his three sons

1966—Bonanza

1967—Bonanza

1968—The Andy Griffith Show: a sitcom about a sheriff, his son (played by Ron Howard), and a bungling deputy (played by Don Knotts)

1969—Rowan & Martin's Laugh-In: a far-out, fast-paced comedy variety show

1970—Rowan & Martin's Laugh-In

1971—Marcus Welby, M.D.: a medical drama starring Robert Young

1972—All in the Family: a hilarious but thought-provoking sitcom about an uneducated and outspoken man, starring Carroll O'Connor.

1973—All in the Family

1974—All in the Family

1975—All in the Family

1976—All in the Family

1977—Happy Days: a nostalgic sitcom featuring a hero who's hip as well as human

1978—Laverne & Shirley: a funny sitcom about roommates who are trying to make something special happen in their lives

1979—Laverne & Shirley

1980—60 Minutes: a magazine format news show

1981—Dallas: a nighttime soap opera, featuring the most unscrupulous character of this era, J.R. Ewing